In *Evaporating Rage*, Norm Mattox's poems seethe with precisely articulated rage and pain.

From police murders to the institutional racism that permeates this country, he eloquently elucidates our desperate need for social and political change. "George Floyd choked to death / on the acid and bile rising in his throat, / mixed with fear hate and racism / blocking his windpipe" (from "positional asphyxia").

The content gradually shifts to an exploration of an inner world that reconciles rage with endurance and resilience. These poems throw out lifelines of hope and appreciation for the wisdom of embracing life in spite of its unpredictability and adversity as in these lines in "from horizon to horizon": "balance your accounts on a full crumb like two slices of life / the past and the future both rising and falling / on both sides of the equal sign."

Read this book to vitalize your spirit and catalyze our fight for justice!

—**Kimi Sugioka, poet Laureate of Alameda, California**


Norm Mattox is a consummate educator with a love for words. He brings us into his laboratory of life, not to create monsters, but to share wisdom. Norm blends his gift of spoken word cadence with biting words inviting us to investigate the lives of people of color in America. A place where we seem doomed to have anything—from a comb, to a phone, to an open palm—be misinterpreted as a deadly weapon, inviting others to take our lives.

Mattox carries us through the Big Bang, leaky logic, biology, mathematics, and fractalization as he speaks of lives too often spent looking for "ground to bury [our] light." But the mitochondrial lineage of ancestors cries out to be heard as we continue to rage against injustice. And Mr. Mattox gives a serious and wholehearted response to that call.

*Evaporating Rage* is filled with hard truths, plaited with love. But, be warned. This is not a book built for a straight through, comfy read with a cup of tea. It must be digested incrementally, in bites, appetizers, and entrees, like all knowledge.

As we stand against "the wailing winds of trauma," seeking to lift ourselves and those we love, while holding onto sanity and humanity, Norm Mattox is a light in this darkness, teaching us along the way that rage can only evaporate when it is fanned with the flames of love.

—**Martina McGowan, author of *i am the rage***

www.blacklawrence.com

Executive Editor: Diane Goettel
Cover Design: Zoe Norvell
Cover Art: «untitled» watercolour on paper, 2022 by Jon Cooper
Book Design: Amy Freels

In June of 2023, Black Lawrence Press welcomed numerous existing and
forthcoming Nomadic Press titles to our catalogue. The book that you hold in
your hands is one of the forthcoming Nomadic Press titles that we acquired.

Published 2024 by Black Lawrence Press.
Printed in the United States.

# evaporating rage

## norm mattox

this collection of poetry is dedicated to the family i was born into, the family that is born from me, and the chosen family of friends, comadres and compadres that have fed me a menu of love and encouragement to "better write that down" through the years of conversation and tears of frustration. this collection is dedicated to the artists and poets that have shared their muses and motivations for their creations that continue to inspire me to observe and listen when the muse whispers in my ear. i am forever grateful.

# Contents

# Foreword

Congratulations. The collection of poems you hold in your hand, *Evaporating Rage*, is one of the most incendiary chronicles of pent-up frustration and anger ever written, the poetic equivalent of *Soul on Ice* written from a more patient perspective, indeed, written with "enough vision to perceive / all the now that needs attention." One would do well to familiarize themselves with the tenets of racial conflict and how that struggle remains deeply unresolved before treading lightly into these pages.

But, also, you hold in your hands the answer to the question that activists and organizers have been asking themselves forever: What do I do with this anger? I won't lie... these answers are not necessarily easy to access, even in this written form. But for those who seek a way through, I can say with the greatest confidence that way is mapped out here, with no greater truth posited than "living Black is an act of resistance."

I can hear many muttering now: What grounds does this fool have to make these bold proclamations? The truth is, I have been as honored and privileged to experience the evolution of Norm Mattox's poetic vision as any other witness of an artist's growth. Norm (or "Math" as Elemen2al The Poet calls him) was working on these poems long before he ever set them down on paper with pen; that is, these poems are imbued with a thoughtfulness that shaped and formed how they would hit before they were born or arranged. A literary work already in progress, Math asked me to work with him not just on this collection, but as editor and publisher of his preceding full-length collection of work, *four crescents*, which serves as a prelude of simmering frustration mixed in a cauldron of collective and individual microaggressions in what is alleged to be a "free society."

as if
the facade of calm
resembles compliance
while it never belies
the toxic burden
of unrequited rage
cooking my guts
into a fricassée

as if
my truth
needed confirmation
by the ones
who never believe
a word i say
anyway

as if
my life
is a problem
that someone else
has a solution for
and love is
the only answer.
                    —From "my Black not blue enough?"

If you recognize the old revolutionary phrase "The left wing and the right wing belong to the same bird" in this work, it's not by accident. The absurdity of racist entitlement comes from all sides of the political spectrum, not just the blatant attempt by MAGA to overthrow this entire conversation in the first place. If *four crescents* is the long-burning fuse, the unsustainable endurance of what is called "polite rage," then *Evaporating Rage* is the explosion followed by the damage and the lingering smoke of that fire.

This poet has salvaged absurdity from hate, laying bare hatred's ridiculous excuses for its own existence in the spin of white nationalist tropes that he turns on their heads to reveal their nakedness. In doing so, he has created a unique satirical voice by recognizing that an honest discussion of race relations must also acknowledge that the anger of the oppressed is a real and tangible thing. If Math's previous collection was thought to be overtly political, then this one is outright polemic, but in a manner that cannot be resisted, much less dismissed:

how many bridges
are burning because
they were built
during bro prez
eight-year regime?

how many fingers
need to be stuck
in amerikkka's eye
because of bro prez's
vision for america
to see, *yes, we can*?

how many mean-spirited bills
need to be passed before
judges start sending babies
back to the state-regulated womb,
treating them like refugees
born in the wrong time?

your threat of a health care plan
weans the sick off the dream
of healing or recovering life
before dying how many times
over a shameless abuse of power?
—From "pointy hoods and red ties"

It doesn't take long for the reader to understand that this is an artist who is also an educator, and that for this particular teacher, the art, and the teaching; the words and the lessons are inseparable. Norm Mattox debunks the myth that the individual cannot be both artist and teacher; indeed, in Math's wake, it becomes difficult to understand how the two could even be separated in the first place.

It is this very twining and/or twinning of the roles of "poet" and "educator" that drives this collection to its unified whole, which is not just an exploration of the effects of rage on the collective and the individual, but also an examination of the aftermath of that rage, as we can see in this excerpt from the poem "life in the in-between":

between making plans            and achieving goals

feeling the blow,
                    absorbing the trauma
                                being knocked down
                                        using gravity to
                                            show
        the strength to rise up
        between being healed of the wound
                                and being cured by
                                    forgiving

The "in-between" of this poem demonstrates an intense mirroring dynamic that plays into the writing of an artist who is all too used to being othered. This dual dynamic is intensified by the pandemic and subsequent quarantine that these poems were forged in, a deep dive into the internal psyche that happened for so many people, not just artists in that time, just before we, as a society, made yet another deep and necessary dive into the politics of civil rights. In the wake of George Floyd, it was no longer just one people of color who found themselves caught between two worlds, but people of marginalized gender and sexual identity, people of labor, and people in need of access who realized the disenfranchisement and erasure of their public voices were subject to the same oppressive forces.

Norm's work over this period, his crafting and polishing of the poems in this book and in *four crescents* is a blow-by-blow reflection of a timeline where heavy restraint, in the name of public safety, is then followed by a pressure valve collapsing and releasing untold energy upon a dormant, if not entirely unsuspecting populace. How to choose between two worlds? The need to be safe was now held in balance with the need to protest; the need to rest and meditate held in balance with the need to connect with others.

But Math, in addition to being a poet, an educator, and a world-class athlete is also a father, and the need for every conscious being to have a place called home underpins so much of the thoughtful rhetoric he lovingly shares with us in these pages. Models of hope emerge from the smoke of creative exorcism—literally in poems with titles such as "ancestral diatribe" and "safe at home"—but also in the meditations that close out this impressive collection, which not only point the way home but provide useful protocols for navigating this traumatized landscape back to sanctuary:

    wake dream keepers
            to bring sage
    where dreams are created
            the same place
    where dreams are treated
            for smoke inhalation

    draft EMTs to heal      the wind
            a siren song     clears a path
    to collect        the bodies

    hire civil engineers to redesign
            labyrinth paths
    to a peace of mind

be gentle   with lives
never   lived like this
  the first time

no muscle memory
to remember how
      to get home safe
in a strange land
            —From "breaking down the pedestal"

    As stated in the beginning of this essay, the way home, the way to peace, will not be easy to access, but the tools and resources necessary are absolutely waiting for you in these pages, as Norm Mattox, with the true touch of a poet, with the same grace and fiery beauty with which he sets the reader alight at the beginning of this book, alights them back down with compassion and love and gentleness in its concluding words. What I'm saying is: buckle up . . . you are in for one hell of a ride here. And it is every bit worth it because you will be changed by the end.

Paul Corman-Roberts, California, 2023

# Introduction

Almost ten years ago, while reading some essays by James Baldwin, I came across this quote: "To be a Negro in this country and to be relatively conscious is to be in a state of rage almost, almost all of the time..." These words resonated with me because delivering instruction from a scripted curriculum was counterintuitive to me and discouraging to the task of learning.

As a bilingual public-school educator, I felt the strain of working within the education system, against the mind-numbing status quo, for the sake of the student's progress and our collective future. Writing my reflections on these internal dilemmas became the bones for poems that comprise the "rage" portion of the work in this collection of poems.

Although injustice and inequity persist, retirement from the education system and writing poetry has helped me to dissipate the pent-up rage that has roiled in my guts for most of my thirty-year professional career.

*Evaporating Rage* documents the tempest of our times and my personal navigation of shifting dimensions to be present and in the moment. Through these poems, I share my encounters with "inner voices" that orient my journey across my "inner verses" in search of love for self and others, joy for the simple things, and peace within the ongoing chaos of our times. I hope the words in my verses encourage others to speak a truth that inspires change in the hearts and actions of those who can make a difference in the systems that impact our communities.

# unalien

african american

never                     both

always                          neither.

never                          neither

always                     both

human being.

# in my shadow

a silhouette
of every Black man
fitting the description
stopped
frisked
questioned
feared for their lives
murdered

perforated     surfaces
mistaken for pores
bullet holes
too many to count

a halo of light
surrounding me
blocks the vision
of their greatest fear
"they thought they saw..."
shadows hiding in their panic
yeah,
they thought i reached
for a loaded comb
to blow my brains out

a shape with edges tattered
by expanding dreams
filled with potential promise
deflating like a balloon

heaven escaping through
multiple gunshot wounds

no last words whispered
no last rights given

an ecosystem beyond
VR headgear
attuned to inner volatiles
trigger rage
taking one last silent knee
infrared images show
both feet on fire
flames burn up my legs

i am fuse and bomb.
i am blown from hell.
my conflagration follows.

a vision of hope    shredded
beyond recognition
another martyr recycled
into the ancestor bin

an uprooted life
returning to roots
nourished by gaiamundo
calibrating the river's flow
feeding my tree of life
all the xylem and phloem
my branches require
to sustain a full canopy

it will appear
i stand on a pedestal
i balance on a mountain of shoulders
surrounded by a village of my ancestors
each one plays their ribcage
like a tambor
my lips read notes
played on my windpipe
a chorus of voices
reciting my life like a mantra

# amerikkka has been infected

malignant strain of ignorance
mutates into virulent thread
undoing decades of evolving tech

progress
is the disintegration of
mind from heart
heart from mind

we regresses to me
ours shrinks to mines

i, me, my
becomes a mantra

he's a contagion all by his damned self!

gotta vote against the virus
in the white house
before it spreads
beyond the senate

this nightmare is contagious
though         some of us
have been asymptomatic
for generations
indeed         most of us
have a natural resistance
and yet
we might need a hope booster
the titer is getting low

experts          work feverishly          to develop
a vaccine          for this virulent strain of fear and hate
overwhelming natural defenses
          already weakened by social distance
taking us further out of touch

betta vote  in  all  elections

ancestors          got their hand on the lever
feel the scale          tip our way

# a life-threatening experience

living Black in this amerikkka
is a life-threatening experience
that
can happen to anyone
that
    is Black
        has red blood
that
    is Black
        has Black friends
that
    is Black
        has white friends
that
    is Black
        has no friends
that
    is Black
        not even Black
Black is Brown

living Brown in this amerikkka
is a life-threatening experience

protest for justice
    is a life-threatening experience
if you Black or Brown
        in this amerikkka

protest a lie
        is a get-home-safe pardon
if you support white supremacy
                  in this amerikkka

protest for justice
protest for peace
protest a lie
protest for a liar
 living Black is an act of resistance
       melanin in your face
       melanin in your soul
is a life-threatening experience
in this amerikkka

## positional asphyxia


. . .

. . .

. . . an attack on *civil society*?
would that be the knee on my neck?

I AM CIVIL SOCIETY

   problem is
no one called for reinforcements when
your partner's knee closed my air supply!
calling on the national guard
just brings a larger knee!

why didn't they call the
national guard on police?
looks like abdication of duty to me
someone gave up caring about safety

   so now
they    got another name for what
they    didn't do to George Floyd
      now
we can suspend disbelief
that all of us witnessed
a recorded *inappropriate restraining technique*

a choke hold (held for too long)
a lynching (that would be gravity's fault)
a fucking murder (by uniform) and

they say GEORGE FLOYD
didn't die from *positional asphyxia*...
   that George Floyd
died of *underlying health issues*

yeah     no!
two underlying health issues
   many of us already live with
and many of us already die from

  one
George Floyd was born
with too much melanin in his armor
(considered a disability in this amerikkka)

  two
George Floyd choked to death
on the acid and bile rising in his throat
mixed with fear   hate and racism
blocking his windpipe

i can't breathe

# the ocean we are drowning in

the tip of an iceberg
treading water in a
swamp of white supremacy
a patriarchal yoke
lounging across
my shoulders

choking on undertow
is getting easier
to *i can't breathe!* in here!

bias-flavored water
pouring through a charcoal filter

how long will it take to be fed up?

these are the word problems
we try to resolve in math class
no answers, just actions

## polite rage

run me off the cliff—
                    Rage.
life ain't never fair—
                    RAge!
the end is always the same—
                    RAGe!!
Can't see through outraged tears—
                    RAGE!!!

holla out the windows—
                    rage
did i say holla? i meant howl—
                    rage

i had to have *the talk*
with twelve-year-old me.
the last human being
i will ever be,   again—
                    rage.
now,
a Black man outraged
by my polite
                    rage!

how do i
ventilate the adrenalin
to roar at the four winds—
rage that won't be denied?
          no way to uncry the tears
        boiling out my eyes
                burning my cheeks.

can't see the road—
                rage                    tears.


        hold the steering wheel     for dear life
enraged                    ·    my polite
                rage
                        is trying to assuage
my self-hating
                rage!!


looking for words to be
                        projectiles
missiles                a caliber that won't fit in any chamber
or          any barrel.
words               swinging sledgehammers.
pen strokes        slash wider        than switchblade jabs
        to make my point.


it worked this time.
other times    it won't        get me home          safe...
if i speak
            without being spoken to
if i show my hands        empty of everything
            except my palms        and
they too        might be mistaken
                        for a comb
            a phone
        a knife
    a gun.


i will feel this way        as long i am Black        in this amerikkka.
    looking in my rearview                followed by my profile.
                will twelve-year-old me
survive my        rage?

## pointy hoods and red ties

all that's missing
are the sheeted horses
and burning crosses
on the white house lawn,
while the GOP hegemony
want to take away
the only *bone* amerikkkan history
ever threw to the Black survivors
of the middle passage,
a voice in the governance by vote,

an obscured ascendancy,
inhibited success
      despite
partisan obfuscation,
and the barely disguised
racial indignity to the Black american,
who is truly african american,
trying to keep america great.

how many bridges
are burning because
they were built
during bro prez
eight-year regime?

how many fingers
need to be stuck
in amerikkka's eye

because of bro prez's
vision for america
to see, *yes, we can*?

how many mean-spirited bills
need to be passed before
judges start sending babies
back to the state-regulated womb,
treating them like refugees
born in the wrong time?

your threat of a health care plan
weans the sick off the dream
of healing or recovering life
before dying how many times
over a shameless abuse of power?

what barren stall
will those *other* babies
wait out their lives
on hold        as they grow old
waiting for souls to die,

flesh withers off the bone,
starved and starving
for life-giving Spirit
and blood of community
by the land of opportunity?

remember we are human and humane
before we are american and amer-arcane!

# a stain on memory

which america
are you remembering was ever great
that you wanna make it great again?
if you're talking about the Great America
where we bring our children
to distract them from the real amerikkka
then, you know the amerikkka i'm talkin' about.

i'm talkin' about the real amerikkka
that has the most wealth in the world
      that can only be balanced
by an overwhelming poverty of Spirit,
you know the real amerikkka
that has corporate individuals
buying up votes
that dis-integrate our human resources
    into gigabytes with no teeth
      chewing the fat off twisted truths,
praised for their bold-faced lies,
      proud to erase hard-fought progress

lowering the floor
so more believe
they've reached the top
while the rest of us know
the basement
has become our ceiling.

# reality has caught up to the nightmare

i can't breathe
dreaming of
being 'over my head'
immersed in the challenges of society

i can't breathe
buried under the weight
of a four-hundred-year-old anvil
planted in my chest

i can't breathe
building strength to swim
against the currents
arms shackled behind my back

i can't breathe
breaching the surface in time
to explode my lungs
with oxygen burning too fast
like a fuse

i can't breathe
unless
in my 'dream becoming a nightmare'
i evolve into a fire-breathing dragon
i don't need your air anymore

the nightmare becomes real life
something's gonna burn

fire
is all
i CAN breathe!

## which look?

that look
of rage will
get you killed.
hands in the air,
they don't care.
down on your knees,
your life's in the breeze.
face down on the ground,
make sure you feel ground down.

phone by your ear,
you may as well listen
to death come at you,
20 bullets in two seconds.

how many times
did they miss when
you fell to the ground?

Brother Diallo got shot
in the bottoms of his feet
not while running away.

overkill?
kill over.

one more time,
*officer feared for their life!*

i can't resist the twisting
in my guts,
tightening knots,
traumatic memories
play over again,
children will
never play again.

i can't resist the instinct
to protect my brain
where my amygdala sits.

i can't resist the bile
rising in my throat.

dog's jaws clench
down on your shoulder,
pain rages in full flight.

don't pull back when
dog yanks like dogs do.

resisting arrest easier than
resisting pain.

i must resist the twitch muscle
doing what twitch muscles do.
a flinch brings steel rain
pouring down on my bulletproof soul,
burning through melanin flesh
like a torch cuts through ice.

*get that look*
*of righteous indignation*
*off your face!*

don't wanna get shot
when pigs shoot
like pigs shoot.
pig might twitch the wrong muscle,
afraid i'm resisting
bein' dead.

# four crescents

imbedded in the palm of your hand     a streak of violence
    yellow flashes
before red pumps     against clenched arteries     feel the pressure
    build     with each
mouthful of mediocrity     a deep swallow of pride     so as not
    to humiliate

tradition of winning 'fixed' by threats     disguised as quid pro
    quo promises     cards dealt
from the bottom of the pile     a clown with a red tie and pointy
    hood     fails to stay hidden
falls out of the deck     during the shuffle     counting on a trump to
    win   over the face card

dog-eared lies exposed to light of truth     lying tongues burn on a
    slow rotisserie   blistered lips
read in the dark     hyena news slithers through     broken tooth
    smiles     barely hide
sneering condescension                    pulled over          wool
    laden eyes

# raised on PTSD


thinking of all the things that occurred at the olympics
in another country...
>how a White athlete played
>>*ugly american*
and got away with it

even
>leaving his comrades behind for crap and consequence
even
>in this amerikkka      White dude
would be called an *asshole jerk!*
maybe even a
>>"get the fuck outta here you *stupid dick*!"
>by the home crowd
while White athlete
>>olympian dick leaves the scene


now project one of our Black athletes
>any age      on all the scenarios
in both places      in the landscape of my mind
>a *safe space*
the Black athlete
>would probably be pummeled in brazil
and found dead or disappeared
>>in the amerikkkas i live in

all of this could happen to me
>being too pensive and imaginative

## my Black not blue enough?

as if
being *good* or *bad*
makes one a *better* victim
like this is a victim competition

as if
suffering
is the measure of
someone's Blackness

as if
my trauma
is forgettable
when that's all
my body remembers

as if
doing time
being on probation
are normal time intervals
between grades
between jobs
between generations

as if
hard times measured
the amount of struggle
overcoming the myth
american dreams sleep
in Black minds

as if
the facade of calm
resembles compliance
while it never belies
the toxic burden
of unrequited rage
cooking my guts
into a fricassée

as if
my truth
needed confirmation
by the ones
who never believe
a word i say
anyway

as if
my life
is a problem
that someone else
has a solution for
and love is
the only answer.

## ancestral diatribe

no one said it was simple
to put your hand on the doorknob
scroll   through the masks you wear
so you can return home alive

revolution is not      a spin through
    your life cycle    a stationary bike
going the speed of breathing
        last breaths

evolution is      change
at the mitochondrial
            layer of consciousness
unknowing       is not enough excuse
to sustain status quo

i believe dawn and dusk are instruction manuals we never read

we think we know
how to live in       the light
        of day
how to be light     in the dark
        of night

emotions   are like unplanned adventures
       mind   plans
            bends time
            plots  a destination
            becomes   a map
            crosses  internal oceans
            gets lost      anyway


love is a journey      we take to find
   our selves
a reflection      an echo
of a love that resounds
   at humanity's core


      when i dare to be powerful
step into vulnerable
      wipe the sweat from my palms
bring unexpected      to status quo
      speak truth to authority
step into the space that needs
my being     not   my doing

## safe at home

when you leave out the door
go          where you're gonna
     go,
do          what you goin' out to
     do,
you just wanna get home safe!

living while Black
               in this amerikkka
getting home safe is
               not a foregone conclusion.

stayin' at home while Black
               in this amerikkka
don't guarantee your safety
                    neither.
uniforms so afraid of my Black
               they shoot through walls
to kill my shadow

     Tryin' to make me disclaim
                    skin i'm in
afraid to wear it on my face.
     eyes showing fear
looks like rage                    can't breathe
                    can't sneeze
               can't cough
     can't wear a mask
to be safe
     in this amerikkka            .
may as well          martyr me Black!

## the boil in the bubble

exploring the differences
by comparisons
of better than,
higher than,
righter than,
whiter than,
dichotomies
causing distances
unsafe for feeling.

easier to see
with blind eyes
that believe only
what can be seen
through closed minds
by robed and covered
perspectives.

watch out for up close
heartfelt beats
that resound with
the earth sounds
rumbling gently,

moving mountains
of oxygen breezes
blowing like hurricanes
outta oceans of trees.
moths and butterflies
amassing like
a san francisco fog
metamorphosing
a summer solstice sun
into a winter solstice
new moon, frigid night.

●  ●  ●

# how to sustain peace

reasons to change
less faith in mind
more faith in chaos
call it faith in life

life is air in a breeze
no force
no direction to change
fills the space with whispers
offers refuge from the noise
mind fills to capacity
impatient waiting on patience
to go with the flow

life is air in a hurricane
a force         has direction
fills space
no refuge
to shelter
to wait life out
resist its flow
at your own peril

mind tells us
we are drowning
if we hold our breath
too long in the dark
eyes open to a desert
no oasis in sight

our mind tells us
demands
that we choose
the *right* direction
to keep up     or be
left behind

life
moves forward
all directions
every instant
a big bang

life
has no place to go in a hurry
doesn't have to make a reservation
to hold space

life
doesn't follow a road map
or chart a path
with a blue star
that marks a destination

life
doesn't demand order
or need a sequence of events
for anyone to arrive
to a better understanding

now is frozen in time
where there is only
heat from friction

moment after moment
barely squeeze through creases in time
perforate invisible barriers
permeated by leaky logic

the kind that makes sense
because it has to

when all it is
is chaos
called by its true name.

# i'm wrestling...

how are you feeling?
     *i'm not! i'm still numb...*
*not paralyzed,*
       though,
stuck   in        between calm and hysterical,
          between facts and feelings,
     between triggers and bullets,
between seconds and lifetimes.

i'm wrestling with telling...
           telling what?
        telling who?
     telling how?
telling when?

i'm wrestling with        telling who when?
     i'm wrestling with       telling who what?
       i'm wrestling with   telling who
                      what
                      when?

     *get my drift?*

it feels like a time for vulnerable strength.
it looks like a time for patience.
         though
it's more like    a time for silent
     primal screams      like prayer...

like a time for strength in faith.
      a time to find strength in vulnerability.

      *i'm glad you asked, so i could be honest.*

## notes to myself

it'sa good thing
i'ma write poetry
to express my outrage.

if not for that and meditation
i'd self-immolate regularly
recomposing myself from ashes.

i'ma stay home
breathe one breath at a time
appreciate simple blessings.

it'sa good thing
i'ma stay *remote* from
community protests.

i don't want to witness or
threaten my life energy
being co-opted by chaotic rage.

emotional boundaries
overrun by stampede
shit happens so off the plan
i'm more concerned
by the mob within
wrestling with my own chaos

death is not incidental to protest.

i have a hard enough time
deciding what to live for.

used to live my life
for my dawtas
planning a life i wanna live
interrupted by other reasons to die.

definitely not safe while
being covertly targeted
for my profile
i have to make amends
with the reaper
live life 40 minutes
in fronna me.

i'ma do my best
to stay safe in my Black man skin
that's the long fight!

ancestors remind me
the ongoing struggle is life!

gotta meditate harder,

write peace i can share.

**over my head**


living life    in    a state
of      being held hostage    by promises
from another lifetime    waiting to be kept

this model created to fail
perfect              in its execution              faulty parts
    sold for parts              fractured tools              building castles of
    sand
in the surf      fabricating dreams    that drown the dreamer

rising tides          erase the blueprints    inky plans dissolving

    history buried under      lies and broken promises
    like treaties      written in the lead of bullets
the blood of sisters and brothers              making us ancestors
    before our time

limbo on the bridge
          between        then          and    now
          between        nightmares    and    real life
          between        history        and    what happens next

hope becomes a rogue warrior        escapes the void
    looking for wounds to heal    remembering where
scars came from              recreating trauma
        to record where    lessons failed        lessons learned

crossing space between stars    wearing a snorkel    exploring the dark
        inner light beams    across      spiraling paths spin off
in all directions          with courageous love

my next strokes                    will find traction and leverage
     against the inertia of fear     oxygen will fuel my next breath
a roar for justice          so future ancestors
          will remember peace

## meditation threads

sitting    straight back    in the wooden desk chair
silent  like meditation    steady breathing
eyes closed    glaring at the back of my eyelids
waiting for the tick tock    calendar pages turn

legs shift    feet shake  as
temperatures rise  and
    feelings    start to boil
slice    like daggers thrown    from
  across the room    aimed at your eyes
can't see them coming

have 'thinking crazies'    afraid of being seen
    hope to be obscured
can't wrap your arms around that    "i know crazy
    this ain't it!    i've wrapped my arms around crazy
all i was hugging    was me!"

push into vulnerability
feel safe enough    to fall into chaos
    walk the fine line between
now  and        never again
  i stand up against    the wailing winds of trauma
gusting cycles of fear
    pain    horror
  sexual exploitation    physical battering
    emotional abuse    psychological triggers
    set like minefields    torched forests
    burned beyond recognition

the body releases its carbon
   every rock overturned
     every wall crumbled

trauma echoes resound  in the silent body
  that mind wears like ill-fitting pajamas
makes us wear PTSD   like calloused skin
  broken bone scars  scarred over

angers break my voice  into fifteen shards of glass wood and
metal bearings  implode inside a vest wearing a mask
  a quarter smile turns into
a dark dangerous terror-filled stare
  target shredded

survivors call for extra band-aids  to tape the tail on the donkey
me feeling like an ass that i grew manhood
out of wild seeds  thrown on fallow macho  tattooed with a
  mustache
expecting tree rings  without nurturing the ground  like
you wanted something to grow

## what you don't have weighs you down

remember when
you had a headache for the first time,
how the lights hurt your eyes
how nausea took away your hunger?

remember when
you heard about the big C,
the thing that could hide
anywhere in your body
and kill you
in the nightmares
of your daydreams?

remember when
you wore fear?
      worry wore your face
like there was something to
      worry about

every sneeze,
      every cough,
      every pain
in my head,

every slow healing scab
was a cancer undiscovered

remember when
i gave up worrying
about dying in
this dimension?

what sense does it make
worrying about dying
while dying doesn't give
two fucks about me?

what lays in fronna me
a path i've never walked
steps   i've never taken
no other   footprints
and yet   all paths before me
lead to the same destination

the challenge is creating life
i haven't imagined
only realizing now
that life is like love
its own flow of chaos

i am a fool thinking
i control destiny
as if faith is under control
while life      threatened
leaves you behind

i choose life
taking me where i need
to be
not like it'sa place i need
to go

# in search of myself

an expedition across  the expanse
   that opens behind my eyelids
      the pause between exhale and inhale
a sliding door timed

to look away  just    before the impulse
to sabotage      the first step      in the journey
   across the innerverse

fear     that i am lost       before i begin
   emotions    congealed in held breaths

fear     that i have not imagined
   the enormity of this quest

there is
no thing to find
   no thing to discover
no thing to claim      at the end of this expedition
  climbing mountains did
not lead to finding any  things

got lost in retreat         searching for
  dust ball    breadcrumbs
   blown asunder with each step

the wake of my passing       closes behind me
  there is no going back
each step      a heart's beat      towards a new home

# like it or not

shelter in place
self-quarantine
an opportunity
to go inside...

maybe build a rocket
            to explore
                    your innerverse

maybe invent the fuel
            for a rocket
                    you've already built

maybe leave your skin
            in a pile at the door
                hand sanitizing raw knuckles

peeling outta gloves
            like a snake
shedding lives
            between a rock
and a hard head

say goodbye to
        superficial thinking
poets are the scouts
        exploring with innervision

## tumbling walls


i want my poems to be timeless
          reality reminds me
      i am barely a glimpse
      of the expression
  of words      especially since
now only reaches
              to the horizons


pages flame with passion
      that consumes a forest
fingertips crumble          like cigar

                    a

                    s

                    h

typing words
      that would blister my lips
and            singe my mustache
if I speak them into ether      must read them
      must hear them read


the form of the stanza      follows
      the curves of my heart      traces
the angles of my bones swinging
on            hangers    in the closet
      on the page      you see the elegance
in my caesura  eyes shift through
blank space      at the intended pace
      the gravity drop      after the
                    line break

while my silent pause
                    makes you uncomfortable
           i'm waiting for the echo of
your last thought to
       land on all the places
              that need to listen


while my profile
                      assumes the mirage of calm
i am the only witness
       to the tremor
    shaking my foundations
         tumbling the walls          and trap doors
that kept me safe    from my self
in the mansion housing my breath


no one imagines the roar
       of traditional pillars     caving inwards from
attic to basement            the internal reclamation of space
repurpose the parts
              redesign the original creation
         longing for a place inside my skin
i can call home

# my mind is a heartless voyeur
## *(keeps love in the basement in a transparent freezer)*


my mind doesn't love me like you do
my mind makes me the lover in the closet
my mind makes me the shadow
   under the  door
my mind makes me the intruder on a *'good thing'*
my mind reminds me, *you are the 'other guy'*!
my mind makes me the **he** that *has to go*!


my mind is indifferent to feelings
   makes me question conditions
i put on  unconditional love
my mind laughs at me behind my back
  scoffs at me with *i told you so* refrains
my mind sounds like a parent
   full of *woulda, shoulda, coulda* advice


my mind does not love me like my heart does
   my mind is outside my self
  full of logic and objective perspectives
anticipates crisis when feelings
   are considered facts  and
thinking is done with the conscience of a heart

conscious feelings                 wrestling with
unconscious thoughts   threaded     through double-eyed needles
              by drunken monkeys

who loves me,   reminds me
        i am more than what my mind thinks
        i am the revolution in my evolution
        i am more than consequences and outcomes
        i am an ongoing sequence of ones and zeroes
        i am a trend of nows that make me present

i risk not knowing      where from   storms blow
        my anchor to love is enough

# sir real

flesh and bone poets     much more
than     beautiful  life saving
spirits giving     volume to voices
zooming  outta the ether
sing     snarling
spitting  swirl
squeezing   wheeze
wailing cries     cringe
crawling words     hum earworm
hymnals     and dance
nap time lullabies

before commas pause the flow
line     breaks     drop
before  pages turn     orphans
leave    to begin   the next chapter

feelings grow flesh
layers of epithelial cells contain spirit
like fully loaded memory     spontaneous
explosions ruin smooth reflections
knee jerk responses threaten
status quo     hopes  superficial
returns to normal     let looks
continue to deceive

## some other times silence

sometimes, we hope for

silence to be the solace

that muffles the babble.


other times, we find

silence in the minefields

planted by blind monkeys.

# life in the in-between

living in the in-between
        neither here             nor there
yet

between making plans     and achieving goals

feeling the blow
        absorbing the trauma
                being knocked down
                        using gravity to show
the strength to rise up

between being healed of the wound
                and cured by forgiving

between the arrogance that comes
with being called an *expert*     and the humility to admit
        how much you don't know
yet

grandma who's my mama
        nietacita quien es mi'ja
              i am none of those names
yet

i am all of my ancestors     the being is     all i'm doing

i am blessed     to be in-between     the universe

        and my innerverse

## mourning interrupted

driving down hill
    you show up in
  the middle
    of a sky    mourning

  careful to stay in my lane
keeping my eyes on you    and the road

i marvel at your balance
    how you hover in the air
  eyes locked on me
    you swoop through my windshield
  arms open wide
    encircle me
hug the air out of my lungs

i must pull off the road
  up on the curb
    you hold me in stupor
try to catch my breath
    recover my sight
eyes swim    no
drown  in a river of tears
  holding on
fiercely to the steering wheel

letting go of the fear
i would never see you again

# if i go first

she will mourn me
until she can curl her ribs
into fingers interlacing a hug
a place she can call home.

true and devoted with
an unquenchable
hunger for love.

as much as
she needs is
as much as
i want to give her.

family gossip whispers
loud enough to hear
she uses me
digs into my silver
waits on my gold.

how wrong they are.

she is chained
to the mine of love
that is mine alone.

arms to hold
breath to breathe
love to fulfill her addiction.

i am the drug
withdrawal will not
undo the mourning.

suffering will be in the
arms of the chauffeur
driving my ashes
to the ocean.

## ashes yearn for company

a partner in life
a trajectory of
happily ever afters

she left with love
she never came home

grief

packed all her smiles
boxes stacked to the ceiling
handwritten labels
block letter kisses
bubble wrapped hugs
closets full of memories

her feet filled those shoes
like a parade of sisters
standing in formation

there's joy in grief knowing that
she's welcome to visit
rude and uninvited on a whim

even though she has her own key
she knocks every time
confident i'll invite her in

fingers hearts eyes
read the card
written in longhand

her shadow
keeps the door   ajar

i've got other things to do
she won't stay
as long as
her light
has a place to stand
under the hat
in the closet
a jar

## i lick the scar
### *(when the wound heals)*


a bruised psyche
  welcomes promised pleasures
  small talk   stokes embers
      to open flame
no love    no third-degree burns
    the scar remains
         hidden under a mute heart
  a heart     yearns for
a refuge
  not a shelter
   a home
    where the ground
   caresses tired soles
 ease the weight off tattered souls
heaven opens to a heart
   empty pours out
  peace fills the shadows
becomes a chamber of love
    open wounds heal from inside out
no space for abscessed thoughts
    a keloid wears courage like a mask
hides resentment   behind a calloused smile
 a scar worn as a badge of honor
      love is at work

**tears**


a levee surrounds my eyes
channels amniotic fluid
through intrafacial aqueducts
and furrowed brows

sight drowns in vision
smooths wrinkles
formed by too much smiling

an emotional moisturizer
keeps complexion supple

lanes of emotion
run down cheeks
taste like an ocean of music
deep enough to drown
in baptismal waters

eyelid lubrication hides
skid marks blinking back
one trauma
that had to be seen
to be believed and
yet unbelievable
simultaneously

like a chord
not an arpeggio llegando
al mismo tiempo
all at once

ahora
now

hearing every note
like a drumbeat
at the desert's edge

better than cocoa butter
on ashy joints

a cathartic shower
to soak in

# what world do we live?

a world struggles around
      how to share emotion
  a desert of wordless feelings
  i show up mute
a blank stare in my eye
   sees passed the rods and cones that
      configure a map to follow

the profile of your smile
  a blurry crease    follows
the faintly flashing    arrows pointing the way
   through the smoke and mirrors
  reflecting    on the first hug
your back curves under my palms
   breathe a deep sigh
let go     of the fear   of letting go

the muse is a potent mentor
  cascading color-coded     themes to scribe
   while the silence is deafening
i can't bear myself       void of voice
no patience   for thoughtless babble
     filling silence       with empty calories
not moving the dial   passed the thunder
    waiting in my chest    a disembodied voice
sings hymnals   live-streamed to the cursor
pulsing     waiting to fill in the blank

# in limbo

the distance
            between
    two                                    stars
            going supernova

            between
        holding on            and            letting go

the time            between
        closing doors            and            doors opening

in limbo

            between
        rational thought            and            feelings

            between
        reality                        and            dreams

            between
        who you think i am            and            who i am
                    i don't think            i am

in limbo

            between
        the human doing            and            the human being

in limbo
  in flux
    in transition

  between
    stopping
    and
    going

  between
to                    and                    from

on the way
    from emptiness
      past fullness
        to wholeness

# a journey across the veil of my flesh

baby toes nibbled like kernels of corn
   on the left foot       fresh peas
      on the right
a perfect landscape
      to show where life has spilled me

a climb up the canopy
   like two saplings'       legs
the one on the right   grew faster   than the one on the left
      launching into a *flèche* attack
the left leg    straight    like the shaft of an arrow
    the body flies   to make a point
   lands like an oak tree   *en garde*

to scale this body  is easier for the shape
   this life has taken     the skin no longer slides
through the air   pockmarks and scars   spaced
like toe holds  used to be     a smooth
steep   vertical    El Capitán body

time has worn the body like a putty knife
     spreading wrinkles       that used

to be curves     the sheen     has lost its
luster     life has chiseled spirit
that shines

     out the back of my eyes

# will we ever hug again?

how will it feel to bow warmly
not knowing if your partner
is bowing at the same temperature
when you can't even see them
bowing so deeply?

will a puddle of tears become a ritual
to demonstrate how long
you stayed in your bow
crying          seeing a loved one
for the last time?

will your child have to crawl
to a spot on the floor
to show how glad
they are to see you?

will mental telepathy
be the new caress
applying creative visualization
chanting a mantra to resonate
the vibe that nourishes spirit?

what about the body that transmits
radiates and absorbs feelings
without the biofeedback that reminds
us    we are one human being
with every one human being?

*what you see is what you get*
could be the new greeting
WYSIWYG scrolls across a blank facade
painting a smile on your mask

will ventriloquism
become a new art form
for whispering *sweet nothings*
into your ear        from six feet away?

will we become
a society of voyeurs
watching others
pleasure themselves
while we do our best to reciprocate?

will a pivot in the psyche
sustain the distance
we are evolved to close?

how long will it take
before i can hold
love in my arms again?

# falling down

soft as down falling
                in-between time
listening to light            crossing shadows

less sound being silent as owl's wing
      a falcon glides          against the wind
              no effort

agitated prey      give them away
        patience
    waits
silent
    senses      heightened
watch     from beyond vision

listen      for stealth
shadows creep    towards dreamscapes
    still enough dusk light
       you can see straight
through creases     in the wind

orange    red      magenta strokes
    paint the horizon
winking stars    call for nightfall

# a mind in touch with a body


a body in touch with itself
a mind is not a body
a mind
needs no body
needs no air
no blood
no feelings

a hand is a body until
it is in touch
with another hand

one hand teaches the other hand
how to hold    to grasp        to caress
the other hand teaches there is
something to lift
something to pull
something to let go of

a foot is a body
until it touches the ground
until it feels the weight
a body standing over it
until the ground with its gravity
pushes against the foot
a call from the body to support it
finding balance in itself
flowing from heel to toes
in concert with falling and

the need for another foot
in contact with gravity
the ground
and a body

a heart is a body
until it is filled with electricity
sparking across synapses
filling with blood and shock
mixing oxygen and food
energy to sustain
a body in touch with itself

a mind is not a heart
never in a body

## weather report

clouds bloom like chrysanthemums
a slow-motion explosion edges
fractaling light refracturing
manufacturing
cultivating moisture
shifting temperatures
sucking water plumes out of thin air
becoming dense
almost impenetrable   not
impervious to gloom-filled grays
shadows dominating underbelly
skies overflowing
water pouring into gravity
falling into chaos
scattering people to find cover
causing disorder
raindrops racing to the ground
heat rising
carrying steam
hot air building up friction
energy bringing the rumble
between       wet     and     dry
between charges      positive  and  negative
until electricity explodes in all directions
looking for ground
burying light
streaking in an instant
not far behind
surrounding   vibrations announce

the parting of bonds
separating particles too fast
light    sound  blind  shiver  shake    walls
tumbling ear drums
echoing underfoot in the puddles
gathering around the auricle chambers
of startled hearts.

gaiamundo loves the dance
between air and water
inundating some
while   only quenching
her thirst     our salvation

# walk in the woods

a wet stormy forest
a pungent feast
for the senses

an aromatic blend
decomposing underfoot
drying herbs

smelling themselves
a persistent menthol
soothes cloistered lungs

recycled water
fresh from the sky

earth's thirst
never quenched

rushing winds
sound like

blowing waves
thundering through
the canopy and understory

a poignant chorus
owls
call and respond

punctuate
the relentless
blowing wind

a reminder
that wings
continue their song
all the same

a disharmonic symphony
of woods
whining
groaning
grinding against
trunk to trunk neighbors

i am drenched with joy
i am an atom
in this gigantic organism

not a witness
nor a bystander
to natural forces of nature
i AM one!

# from horizon to horizon

enough vision to perceive
     all the now that needs attention

futures swim like squid      fly like arrows through
       a virtual *no place*

a wandering mind shifts with currents
trends trail off into distracting vibrations

the past beyond the horizon   an anchor     a sense of security
neither good nor bad   at least    a known quantity
no variables to juggle   results achieved   outcomes accounted for

now   demands too much   attention to pay
when is life lived   or     is persistent being in life
called living

balance your accounts  on a full crumb   like two slices of life
     the past and the future   both rising and falling
        on both sides of the equal sign
the present       full of indescribable flavors

now   full of ingredients to live       completely

# breaking down the pedestal

the tide
     a border in motion
a swirl of yellow flags
       warnings wash up in the rocks

i entertain overnight overtures
  at the mouth of the bay
      time limited to blueprints
drawn on waterproof paper

where to build home
      futures subject
to sea changes
   rip currents   undermine
dreamy loam foundations

without vision  hope
   at risk of sliding into
the surf
      undercurrents
          undercut
      underground
fiber optic images
        of designer dreams

too many shadows
     in the light of dusk
timing reality       a hazard

a moat malfunction      signals
      fear      on high alert
      encoded messages
scroll across chicken skin

status quo guardians      suggest
you bring kindling  lay it at the foot
of unfinished bridges      suggest
you collect tinder   not blankets
            for cold hearts

wake dream keepers
            to bring sage
where dreams are created
            the same place
where dreams are treated
            for smoke inhalation

draft EMTs to heal      the wind
      a siren song   clears a path
to collect         the bodies

hire civil engineers to redesign
      labyrinth paths
to a peace of mind

be gentle   with lives
never   lived like this
   the first time

no muscle memory
to remember how
            to get home safe
in a strange land

# anticipation

what sound do you hear at the end of a breath?
    the churn of your wonder
the confluence of your essence meeting life
    a jumble of harmonic
        resonant chaos off horizons colliding


bated breath        the panic
    heart beating
        no
          beats skipping
to catch up    to the rhythm of memories
    you just remembered...    from another lifetime


a foreign agent    preparing to invade
        your under-minded chambers
closet walls    about to be caved in    by
    the torrent of images
        no
    words describing images
you've never seen    never existed
    until they met the borders
    collapsing at the end
        no

the beginning of thoughts          you never thought before

time to wake from the slow motion
                              binge reel of life
          spooling before your eyes
                    in the moments before the next breath
if you decide to never                         breathe again

# in time for life

awareness moves through a string of nows
with confident agility
time moves straight
like windblown dandelion seeds
forward endlessly
sometimes
slow enough that
time appears to stop
but doesn't
we barely keep pace
we are usually behind
we get distracted by things
become attached to things
fall behind time's pace
sounding alarms go off on
someone else's scheduled
event canceled

when someone cautions,
*don't get ahead of yourself*
is there *another* you out there
moving slower?
how does this person know

the pace *another* you moves
when you didn't know there was *another* you?
describe the *standing still* sensation of time
what's the difference between time and life?
sense time *standing still*
life moving forward at the same pace as time
life *runnin' neck and neck* with time
to meet up where you are

the absolute reason for the fencer's exaltation
the explosion, the score
the *et la!* roar
when *la belle touché*
*the beautiful touch* is scored
*et la* is french for *it's there!* or *there it is!*
a convergence in life
a point scored by a line
established in time

life's complexities
mind synthesizes experiences with life
awareness like an epiphany
acknowledgement of totality in the instant

but i digress…

life is the laboratory
where awareness, and thought
decompose variables
such that
action comes through
the marrow of human existence

life comes from all directions
life goes in all directions
multiple layers of relevance
concentric spheres configured
like rings of saturn
around the core of who you think you are

some spheres dense enough
they have personality
thoughts of their own
charismatic enough to attract strangers
maybe not enough gravity to keep friends

fragile spheres thin
like eggshells
fracture under stress
breaking down so easily
when they looked so solid
enduring little past the first knock

ingenuity  opacity  invisibility  clarity

the dance between the lens and focal point

what you're looking for

find it by its missing

look for nothing

see more

## evaporating light

fading light
looking for a rainbow
an ache in the sky
evaporating like drops

hearts of light
find your place in the arc
keep singing no matter
how dark the clouds

# Acknowledgements

The following poems have been shared in a collection titled *four crescents* published by Collapse Press: "ashes yearn for company," "breaking down the pedestal," "ancestral diatribe," "my mind is a heartless voyeur," "mourning interrupted," "if i go first," and "tumbling walls." Individually, all of the poems in this collection have been shared in virtual open mics, nationally and internationally, because of pandemic restrictions.

I would like to extend heartfelt thanks to the Nomadic Press community of writers and poets who have inspired and nurtured my creativity by example, by challenge, and in deed. The spaces we collaborate in are brave and safe for our trusting one another and finding strength in our vulnerable truths. I am grateful to the SF Creative Writing Institute and their cadre of instructors who mentor and challenge the creative processes. With their regular generative workshops, RoblesWrites Productions and Art Defined Productions have been instrumental in my differentiating and developing the volume in my voices.

Norm Mattox is a poet. He served as a bilingual educator in the public school system of San Francisco Unified School District for over 30 years. Though retired, Norm is a teacher ('maestro' in Spanish) for life. His poetry is a journey through the voices that tell a story of love in a time of struggle and challenge. Norm has shared his poetry as a featured reader, at open mics around the San Francisco Bay Area, select venues in New York City and other parts of the world across the 'zoom universe'. Norm's poetry has been published in two chapbooks. His first collection is titled, *Get Home Safe, Poems for Crossing the Community Grid*. Norm's second chapbook length collection is titled *Black Calculus*, published in 2021 by Nomadic Press. An audiobook by the same title was released in 2021. Collapse Press published Norm's third poetry collection, *four crescents,* in 2023.